Colorful Days

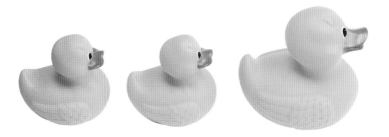

Días de colores

FIRST EDITION
Series Editor Deborah Lock; **Senior Art Editor** Tory Gordon-Harris; **Design Assistant** Sadie Thomas;
Production Claire Pearson; **DTP Designer** Almudena Díaz; **Jacket Designer** Peter Radcliffe;
Reading Consultant Cliff Moon, M.Ed.

THIS EDITION
Editorial Management by Oriel Square
Produced for DK by WonderLab Group LLC
Jennifer Emmett, Erica Green, Kate Hale, *Founders*

Editors Grace Hill Smith, Libby Romero, Michaela Weglinski; **Spanish Translation** Isabel C. Mendoza;
Photography Editors Kelley Miller, Annette Kiesow, Nicole DiMella;
Managing Editor Rachel Houghton; **Designers** Project Design Company;
Researcher Michelle Harris; **Copy Editor** Lori Merritt; **Indexer** Connie Binder;
Proofreaders Carmen Orozco, Larry Shea; **Reading Specialist** Dr. Jennifer Albro;
Curriculum Specialist Elaine Larson

Published in the United States by DK Publishing
1745 Broadway, 20th Floor, New York, NY 10019
Copyright © 2023 Dorling Kindersley Limited
DK, a Division of Penguin Random House LLC
23 24 25 26 10 9 8 7 6 5 4 3 2 1
001-336813-Aug/2023

A catalog record for this book
is available from the Library of Congress.
HC ISBN: 978-0-7440-8377-4
PB ISBN: 978-0-7440-8376-7

DK books are available at special discounts when purchased in bulk for sales promotions, premiums,
fundraising, or educational use. For details, contact: DK Publishing Special Markets,
1745 Broadway, 20th Floor, New York, NY 10019
SpecialSales@dk.com

Printed and bound in China

The publisher would like to thank the following for their kind permission to reproduce their images:
a=above; c=center; b=below; l=left; r=right; t=top; b/g=background

Shutterstock.com: Africa Studio 25t, Gunnerchu 4bc, Happy Hirtzel 26-27, Songdech Kothmongkol 11c

Cover images: *Front:* **Dreamstime.com:** Allegro7 cla, crb, Benchart, Raman Maisei cra;
Back: **Shutterstock.com:** Fantastic Day cla, robuart cra

All other images © Dorling Kindersley
For more information see: www.dkimages.com

For the curious
Para los curiosos
www.dk.com

Colorful Days

Días de colores

Elizabeth Hester

Come and play with me.

Ven a jugar conmigo.

How many colors
can you see?

¿Cuántos colores ves?

white

blanco

We can play in the cold, white snow.

Podemos jugar en la nieve fría y blanca.

We can look at the purple flowers.

Podemos mirar las flores moradas.

purple

morado

We can run around the trees that have pink blossoms.

Podemos correr alrededor de los árboles de flores rosadas.

pink

rosado

gray

gris

We can play with
the small, gray rabbits.

Podemos jugar con los
pequeños conejos grises.

We can look at the boats on the blue sea.

Podemos ver los botes en el mar azul.

blue

azul

We can play near the tall, yellow sunflowers.

Podemos jugar cerca de los altos girasoles amarillos.

yellow

amarillo

orange
anaranjado

We can eat a frozen orange treat.

Podemos comer una golosina congelada anaranjada.

red

rojo

We can kick the red leaves. We can also pick the red apples.

Podemos patear las hojas rojas. También podemos recoger rojas manzanas.

black

negro

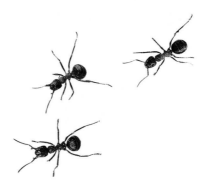

We can look
at the black ants.

We can see the
black beetle.

Podemos mirar las
hormigas negras.

Podemos ver el
escarabajo negro.

We can croak like
the small, brown frogs.

Podemos croar
como las pequeñas
ranas marrones.

brown

marrón

We can walk by the tall, green trees.

Podemos caminar junto a los altos árboles verdes.

green

verde

We can hang up silver balls and put on gold crowns.

Podemos colgar bolas plateadas y ponernos coronas doradas.

silver and gold

plateado y dorado

silver
plateado

gold
dorado

How many colors can you see?

¿Cuántos colores ves?

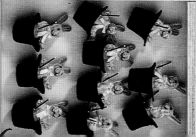

Glossary
Glosario

 blue
the color of some toy cars, blueberries, and the sea

 green
the color of pine trees, tree frogs, and some parrots

 orange
the color of pumpkins, carrots, and oranges

 red
the color of some leaves, apples, and holly berries

yellow
the color of bananas, lemons, and sunflowers

 amarillo
el color de las bananas, los limones y los girasoles

anaranjado
el color de las calabazas, las zanahorias y las naranjas

azul
el color de algunos autos de juguete, los arándanos y el mar

 rojo
el color de algunas hojas y manzanas, y de las bayas del acebo

 verde
el color de los pinos, algunas ranas y algunos loros

Quiz
Prueba

Answer the questions to see what you have learned. Check your answers with an adult.

What color is each of these things?

1. Some blossoms on trees in the spring
2. Some small, fuzzy rabbits
3. Some ants and beetles
4. Small frogs that blend in with leaves
5. A crown

1. Pink 2. Gray 3. Black 4. Brown or green 5. Gold

Responde las preguntas para saber cuánto aprendiste. Verifica tus respuestas con un adulto.

¿De qué color son estas cosas?

1. Algunas flores que brotan en los árboles en la primavera
2. Algunos conejos pequeños y peluditos
3. Algunas hormigas y escarabajos
4. Unas pequeñas ranas que se confunden con las hojas
5. Una corona

1. Rosadas 2. Grises 3. Negros 4. Marrones o verdes 5. Dorada